Advance Praise for
Spiritual Ink

Shannon utilizes her rich experiences as a Child Life Specialist to inspire her readers. Truly an eloquent and meaningful read for a vast audience. As a long time Child Life Specialist, I would highly recommend.

—*Kimberly Eury Allen*, **MS, CCLS, Child Life Specialist**

Spiritual Ink offers a meaningful outlet for expression for those coping with life's challenges. As a Child Life Specialist supporting families dealing with illness, trauma, and loss, I find this to be an invaluable resource that I highly recommend.

—*Shani Thornton*, **MS, CCLS, Child Life Mommy**

Shannon will open the eyes of your heart to see the creativity that lies inside of you. She will help you release emotions that have long held you back. These stories will prompt you to see God in a fresh light and understand that He is with you. God's word comes alive as she has a unique way to incorporate it into digestible lessons of hope for everyday.

—*Jennifer Jackson*, **Radio Show Host of *Simply for Women***

Spiritual Ink is a beautifully written collection of personal essays highlighting the experiences of Shannon's work as a Child Life Specialist. I was moved by her powerful testimonies of children and families and caregivers who play such a pivotal role in her faith journey as well as her personal growth. Shannon discovers profound spiritual treasures and *Spiritual Ink* will inspire you to take a closer look at your own life experiences to find a deeper significance in your interactions and choices while you grow in awareness of God's presence and promises.

—*Christine Carter*, **Author of *Help and Hope While You're Healing: A Woman's Guide Toward Wellness While Recovering from Injury, Surgery, or Illness***

Spiritual Ink is a reaffirmation of faith over fear. The inspiring stories remind you to count your blessings. The benefits of prayer shine brightly in the calm and refreshing words. This book is a recommended read for all, especially for my colleagues in the medical profession, whose souls just need a reminder of what angels truly are.

—*Shelly Fitzpatrick*, **RN**

I love Shannon's books! This book will bring you so much peace, hope and joy even in the midst of having a loved one in a hospital. Her books share how each of us can be God's instruments of joy even in the midst of suffering and pain. Every chapter has a wonderful truth and joy to it. I believe it will bless you as much as it has blessed me.

—*Sally Burke*, **President of Moms in Prayer International**

In *Spiritual Ink,* Shannon Alford beautifully blends spirituality and creativity into a powerful narrative that speaks to the heart and soul. Her words are a gentle invitation to reflect on the deeper meanings of life, offering insight into how our faith and artistic expression shape who we are. Shannon's unique perspective inspires readers to explore their own spiritual paths while embracing the creative power that lies within us all. Thought-provoking and deeply moving, this book will resonate with anyone seeking a deeper connection between their inner self and their spiritual needs. I highly recommend it!

—*Laurie Hallas*, **Retail Merchandiser and Product Reviewer**

These stories provide such beautiful insight into the "little ways" God shows us His love when it is needed most. Through my journey of love, grief, and the loss of my child, there were countless instances where this could be seen, if only I kept my heart open. Shannon Alford and the other Child Life Specialists were a blessing in my life during those days in that they helped us to notice these moments and hold space for the joy. I pray that these reflections help you to recognize all the "little ways" God is caring for you.

—*Mother of a child with a congenital heart defect*

Spiritual Ink

STORIES TO SPARK YOUR SOUL

SHANNON ALFORD

Book Design & Production:
Columbus Publishing Lab
www.ColumbusPublishingLab.com

Copyright © 2025 by Stars in the Sand Publishing

All scripture quotations are taken from the
New International Version of the Bible.

All rights reserved.

This book, or parts thereof, may not be
reproduced in any form without permission.

Paperback ISBN: 978-1-63337-891-9
E-Book ISBN: 978-1-63337-810-0

Printed in the United States of America
1 3 5 7 9 10 8 6 4 2

To my husband, Ed, and my daughter, Audrey; the people who most spark my soul

Contents

Introduction	1
1. Stars in the Sand	3
2. Don't Miss God	7
3. The "church" of the ER	11
4. Physician in Training	15
5. Love in Action	19
6. Vacation Plans	23
7. Whooshing Prayers	27
8. Little Bird	31
9. Feeling Tall	35
10. Agents of the Day	39
11. Elevator Going Up	45
12. A Library of Memories	49
13. Angels on Call	53
14. Merry & Bright	57
15. Champagne Friends	63
16. X-Ray Vision	69
17. Holy Ground	73
18. Shining Stars	77
19. The Magic of Music	81
20. Here to Help	85
21. Drawn to Healing	89
22. Good Medicine	95
23. Matters of the Heart	99
24. Mental Jewelry	105
25. A Heart of Compassion	111
26. Betty Crocker	115
27. Pray Big	119
28. Flourish	123
29. The Journey Onwards	127
30. Child Life Bro	131
About the Author	135

It is sown a natural body,
it is raised a spiritual body,
If there is a natural body,
there is also a spiritual body.
1 Corinthians 15:44 (NIV)

• •

You show that you are a letter from Christ,
the result of our ministry,
written not with ink but with the Spirit
of the living God, not on tablets of stone
but on tablets of human hearts.
2 Corinthians 3:3 (NIV)

Suggested companion guide from the author

Available worldwide
wherever you buy your books!

Introduction

Big moments happen in hospitals; life changing moments. Hospital work introduced me to a wide range of people and situations throughout the hospital from the emergency department to intensive care. The human experience is a complex one. We are body, soul, and spirit and to be well, sick people need more than physical healing for their bodies. They also need to be listened to, respected, and encouraged. Many of the stories that have influenced me have been through my work as a Child Life Specialist helping children and families struggling with trauma, illness, and loss.

In the rhythm of life, we don't often know what moments will be etched in our hearts and minds. Our experiences shape us and our memories highlight the people and the things that are important to us.

Caring for the sick, hurt, and suffering is important and challenging work. As human beings, eye contact is the primary mode of communication. As a patient's grandmother said, "The doctors aren't God, but God is everywhere here." Each individual's life is powerful but when it's combined with others working towards a common goal, such as helping the sick or hurting, that radiating healing energy can be felt.

Each one of us has an incredible capacity to use our personal scope of influence to make a difference for good in the world around us. Every day at work I got to see examples of this in action. Like a dry plant revived after it's been watered, I saw the effects of weary and discouraged people being uplifted after positive and caring interactions.

"Spiritual Ink" was a name given to me in a dream many years ago. I understood the dream meant that it was to be a book title but I didn't know what the words meant. It was a mystery. Later, clues were revealed to me until I came to understand the meaning that Spiritual Ink represents that each interaction, both verbal and nonverbal, leaves an etch on our human hearts. This book is a collection of some of the meaningful interactions and moments that have made an impression on me.

I also created a resource called *Spiritual Ink Journal, Writing Prompts to Spark your Soul,* which can be used as a companion to this book or used independently.

Having a sick child is stressful and disruptive for the whole family. For this reason, I wrote a devotional for parents of hospitalized children called *Hospital Prayers, A Devotional for When Your Child Needs Blessings & Bandaids.* This resource is meant to offer encouragement and hope during uncertain times.

In each and every day, may you be blessed to find moments of joy, purpose, and meaning.

1.
Stars in the Sand

My husband, Ed, and I celebrated one of our wedding anniversaries at St. John in the Virgin Islands. We spent the days exploring the island and visiting beautiful beaches. At night, we walked on Cinnamon Bay Beach and watched the stars. They were abundant and bright.

The longer we looked up into the night sky, the more apparent it became there were countless smaller stars twinkling near the larger ones. They encompassed the entire sky. A gentle wind was blowing and the soothing sound of waves serenaded us in the darkness. It possessed a beauty completely different than it did during the day.

The sand was soft under our feet and my husband bent down to sift some in his hands. As he did, we were surprised to see little glowing lights in the sand. Like the stars in the sky, some of the glowing lights in the sand shone brighter than others.

Most were green, but some were bluish in color. Ed identified them as plankton. He said he knew they could be seen illuminated traveling behind boats in the water at night but he didn't know they could be seen on land.

I joined him in parting the sand to discover more glowing lights that looked like fireflies. They were everywhere. I commented that they were like stars in the sand.

Spiritual Ink

The presence of stars in the sky and stars in the sand remind me of God's blessings. Some shine brightly and are apparent. Others are hidden away, out of sight, until they are discovered.

The world is full of wonder. Plankton glowed in the sand before our awareness of it. The God who created plankton for his pleasure invited us to share in it, too.

We continued walking silently hand in hand under the starlit night looking out over the ocean, listening to the waves. We had the entire beach to ourselves until a few minutes later when a group of four children ran our way from the other direction.

We exchanged greetings and they briefly paused to show us their discovery. The boys in the group held out their hands to show us glowing green and blue lights on their hands and arms, elated with their findings. We thought our night couldn't get any better but the laughter of happy children enhanced it.

All of earth sing praises to God and that night on the beach, we walked in nature's concert.

**The heavens declare the glory of God;
the skies proclaim the work of his hands.
Day after day they pour forth speech;
night after night they reveal knowledge.
They have no speech, they use no words;
no sound is heard from them.
Yet their voice goes out into all the earth,
their words to the ends of the world.
In the heavens God has pitched a tent for the sun.**
Psalm 19:1-4

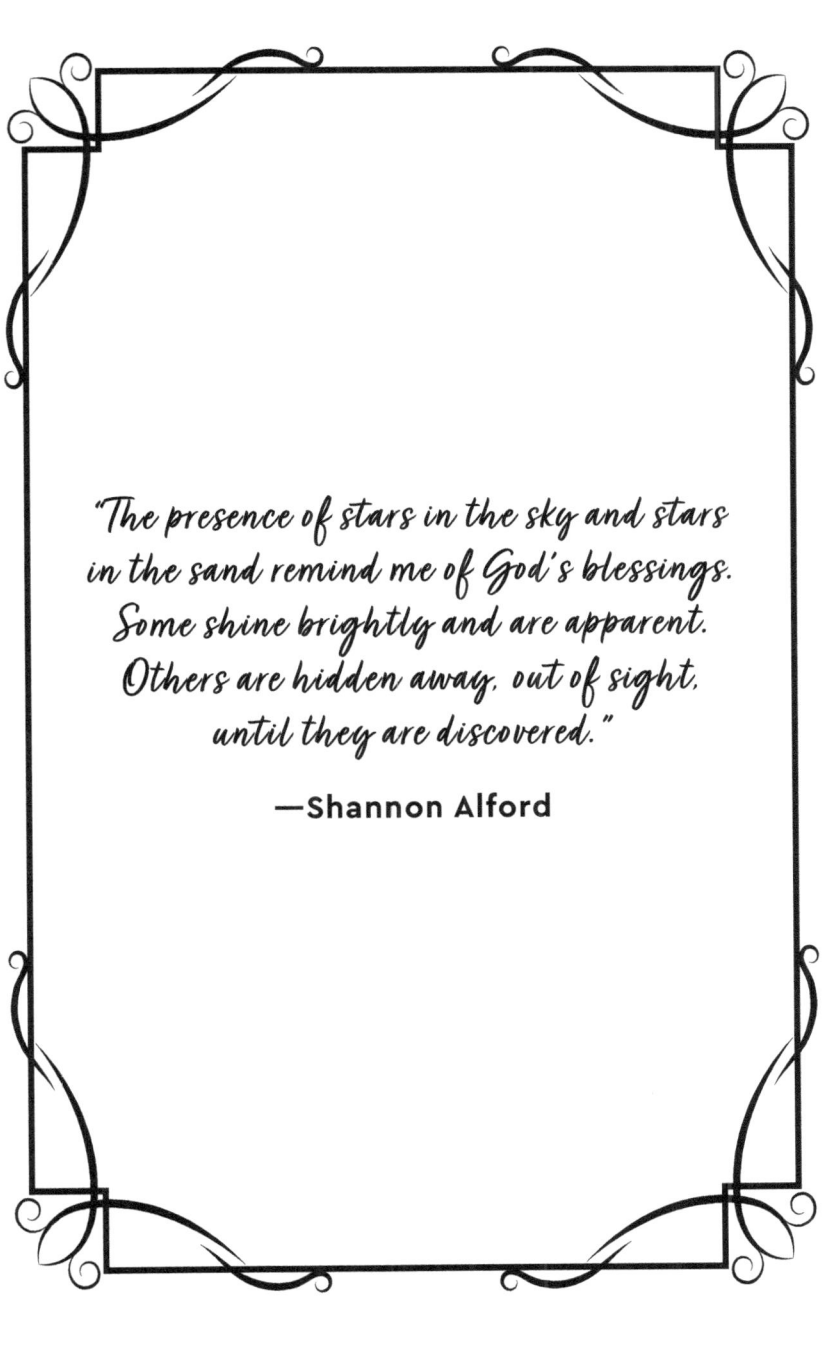

"The presence of stars in the sky and stars in the sand remind me of God's blessings. Some shine brightly and are apparent. Others are hidden away, out of sight, until they are discovered."

—Shannon Alford

2.
Don't Miss God

When my daughter, Audrey, was young, I worked a few evening shifts a week in a pediatric emergency department as a Child Life Specialist. I also babysat part-time for a co-worker's two-year-old, Jillian.

One day when the girls were playing in the front room, I informed the children that it was time for lunch. Audrey went to the kitchen and sat down at their little table. Jillian was usually right behind her. I walked to the front room to check on her when suddenly Audrey called out from the kitchen, "Jillian! Don't miss God!"

Jillian quickly put her toy down on the floor and ran past me and into the kitchen as fast as her chubby little legs could carry her. She rushed into her chair and then in unison they folded their hands, bowed their heads, and prayed, "God is great, God is good, let us thank Him for our food. Amen." It was hard for me to keep from laughing while I joined them in prayer and thought about the wisdom of my five-year-old: "Don't miss God." Life can become busy with many things clamoring for our time and attention. Sometimes I forget that God is in our midst. He is Spirit. His presence is with us because He promises he will never leave us. Taking a moment to remember and appreciate God's nearness helps me to receive his guidance more clearly so I don't miss it.

Audrey and Jillian talked and laughed their way through lunch and I enjoyed watching over them and hearing their conversation. Then I realized God was doing the same with us, smiling and listening. It was a message He didn't want me to miss.

Jesus said, "Let the little children come to me, and do not hinder them, for the kingdom of heaven belongs to such as these."
Matthew 19:14

"Who's God's wife?"

—**My daughter's question when she was young**

3.
The "church" of the ER

A friend of mine once remarked how people tend to devote time and attention in setting goals and making positive changes in areas of personal growth such as: health, fitness, finances, and career, while focus on spiritual growth is often overlooked. I understand how that can happen, because I had experienced the same thing myself in my younger years when I didn't go to church, read the Bible, or nurture my faith. My relationship with God was stagnant and immature.

Once I began working in the ER (emergency room or ED, emergency department) and dealing with life and death situations on a frequent basis, I was challenged by the things I heard and saw. It became clear to me in new ways that the unseen supernatural realm was every bit as real as the physical realm. My spiritual senses began to awaken to a deeper level.

Working with so many people in a fast-paced environment with such a diversity of personalities, skill sets, and situations was a catalyst for accelerated learning and growth. The experienced clinicians I worked with had a wealth of knowledge. They had the ability to medically evaluate patients, but could also "read the room" to quickly assess the dynamics before determining how to proceed. This was especially evident during trauma alerts, when decisions needed to be made quickly. It required an attitude of readiness to respond to any situation and a willingness to observe, listen, and learn. One of the nurses told me that after he completed nursing school, he was excited to work in emergency medicine but five years later, he realized not only how much he had learned, but how much more there still was to know. This is such a healthy attitude to have because learning is an active process that keeps us curious and engaged in our daily pursuits.

One of the stories that influenced me and increased my spiritual awareness was told to me by my friend, Linda. She said that during her orientation as a new nurse in the ER, she was caring for a trauma patient who was initially unresponsive. The patient was revived and then was transferred from the ER to the PICU (Pediatric Intensive Care Unit). The next day, Linda, and a few others involved in the girl's care went to visit her in the PICU. The patient looked a lot better and she thanked them for taking good care of her. The patient explained that she could see how hard they were working because she was watching them from above, from the visual point of the ceiling at the head of the gurney. She also told the resident where his missing stethoscope was. He had not been able to find it in the trauma room the day before. The girl explained to the resident that it was in the pocket of his white physician's coat which was hanging on a hook behind the trauma room door and that's exactly where he found it when he returned to the ER.

We never know what's going to shape us; our spiritual journeys are as individual as we are. In the "church" of the ER, there is a high regard for the sanctity of life. Humanity is connected. We are part of other people's stories and they are a part of ours.

There were many times I had been in trauma rooms with patients but hearing this patient's account brought new awareness which influenced my spiritual growth and clinical practices. There is so much we can learn from one another. The truth of this girl's message resonated deep within me. She spoke of the reality of physical and spiritual realms and the importance of caring for one another. Attunement with God and with other people is what brings great meaning to us in each new day.

God speaks to us in ways we can understand. He spoke to me through my friend's story and through my work in the ER and our relationship grew from there. God's love for us is deep and personal. Zephaniah 3:17 calls God the Mighty Warrior who saves and it also says He delights in us and rejoices over us with singing. God's love is eternal and so is our purpose. He sings over us and gives us each a beautiful song to sing with the stories of our life. Sing on!

You show that you are a letter from Christ, the result of our ministry, written not with ink but with the Spirit of the living God, not on tablets of stone but on tablets of human hearts.
2 Corinthians 3:3

*"Life is a gift;
it shouldn't be taken for granted."*

—**A hospital chaplain**

4.
Physician in Training

During one busy afternoon in the ER, I was paged to the front desk by a unit clerk who told me that I had some visitors. She indicated to a smiling boy and his mom who were waiting for me.

I didn't recognize them at first until the mother explained that they had been in the ER recently when her son was diagnosed with diabetes. Seven-year-old Jayden had been very sick and scared when I met him. He was crying, afraid of injections, and overwhelmed by everything that was happening to him. His nurse had paged me and we worked together to answer his questions and gain his cooperation to help care for him.

Child life specialists often use medical play to help explain information in developmentally appropriate ways. Medical play is a way to help children process their feelings and practice coping strategies to help them manage their anxiety and fears. It gives them understanding and control in an otherwise uncontrollable situation.

Jayden's mom and our staff saw a big difference in this boy after he was given an opportunity to play and recover emotionally. By the time Jayden left the ER for admission to an inpatient unit for further treatment, he was feeling better physically and emotionally, which we were all glad to see.

Standing across from me at the front desk, his mom told me that they had just come from a clinic appointment at the hospital. Jayden had insisted that they stop by the ER before they went home so he could see the lady "who helped kids not be afraid." She didn't know who he was talking about since they had met so many people involved in his care, but the unit clerk knew right away that he was referring to me, the only child life specialist employed in the ER at the time.

Jayden thanked me for helping him and wanted me to know that he was doing okay with the shots. He said he didn't like them but was taking them and he was feeling better. He looked a lot better too.

Working as a child life specialist always reminded me of the story of the boy and the starfish. There are several variations of this story but as it was told to me, there was a man who was walking on a beach after a storm where thousands of starfish had washed up on the shore. He noticed a boy bending down to pick up a starfish and throw it back into the ocean as he walked along. The man asked the boy what he was doing and the boy explained he was returning them to the ocean so they wouldn't die. The man responded by saying that there were too many for the boy to save, but the boy bent down, picking up another starfish and threw it back into the ocean. He turned to the man and said, "It made a difference to this one."

Patient needs exceed the availability of child life resources, but it all makes a difference. Child life specialists have a wide range of skills and responsibilities and flexibility is an essential component of the profession. Interviewing and training volunteers was another aspect of the job.

One year when I helped interview groups of teenagers for the volunteer program, a young man came up to me and introduced himself. He told me that we had met before, in the ER, when he was seven-years-old and was diagnosed with diabetes. It was Jayden.

Jayden told me he was doing well and was excited to volunteer at the hospital. He was planning to go to medical school, and wanted to be a Physician. I felt so honored that he remembered me and was kind enough to talk to me. I'm glad to have met him and for the impression he has left on me. His destiny is great before him.

May the favor of the Lord our God rest on us; establish the work of our hands for us- yes, establish the work of our hands.
Psalm 90:17

"Are the surgeon's hands steady?"

—A seventeen-year-old's question prior to his heart surgery

5.
Love in Action

Many years ago, working on a typically busy night in the ER, I met a foster mom who made an impression on me. She was an older woman who had two little girls with her.

ER visits tend to take a long time because of so many patients needing to be seen. As I stopped back to the patient room to check on them, we became engaged in conversation.

She explained the preschooler was one of her grandchildren and the sleepy toddler sitting on her lap was a foster child.

She had lived most of her life in New York City and she and her now deceased husband had cared for a total of twenty foster children in addition to having children of their own. She was still close to many of them and the little girl in her care would be the last child she fostered, but she was hoping and praying she would soon be a grandchild.

One of her daughters still lived in New York with her husband and children. They were in the process of trying to adopt the toddler, so she could stay with the only family she had ever known.

This woman's love of children was obvious and one of the things she said to me was, "All children are ours." She said children were entrusted to us by God to care for them and guide them. Her words have always stayed with me, and though I don't remember her name, I will never forget her.

> **Speak up for those who cannot speak for themselves, for the rights of all who are destitute. Speak up and judge fairly; defend the rights of the poor and needy.**
> *Proverbs 31:8-10*

"Children were entrusted to us by God to care for them and guide them."

—**A foster mom in the ER**

6.
Vacation Plans

Occasionally at work I unexpectedly saw people I knew who were either there with their child or visiting a patient.

One evening while working in the ER, I saw a familiar face in the cafeteria during my dinner break. He was someone I hadn't seen in years and I had met him and his wife through a friend from college. They lived in a town about an hour away.

We visited for a few minutes and he told me their five-year-old daughter was spending the night after having a tonsillectomy earlier that day. He said she was sleepy and sore but was doing well. This was her first hospitalization and they had not known what to expect. He appreciated she only needed minor surgery instead of something more serious because it was stressful enough having a child hospitalized for any reason. I mentioned I would try to stop by their room to visit if I could.

When I arrived at their room a little while later, his daughter was sitting on the bed. They said she had liked helping to pack her suitcase before leaving. She especially liked having a big playroom located across from her hospital room and being able to order popsicles and ice cream.

I received a card at work from them after their stay and they said on the drive home the next day, their daughter called out from the back seat, "Thanks for the bay-cation!"

> **A cheerful heart is good medicine,
> but a crushed spirit dries up the bones.**
> *Proverbs 17:22*

> *"Some things are kind of fun and kind of scary."*
>
> —An eight-year-old patient after receiving sutures in the ER

7.
Whooshing Prayers

The early years of my ER work were especially exciting and challenging but a downside was that all the exposure to sickness and loss led me to do what came naturally, which was to worry. While I was at work I felt engaged and productive, but at home I experienced waves of anxiety about the uncertainties and difficulties of life. The intensity of working evening shifts often resulted in restless nights and the lack of quality sleep contributed to my anxiety. But somewhere along the way, this cycle of stress began to subside and I realized that I had begun to pray and see responses to that prayer. It started with an inclination to say short, silent prayers for the patients I was with, especially during medical procedures. These quick prayers made me feel calmer and a sense of peace accompanied it. God comforted me and I was better able to comfort others.

Prayer is simply talking to God and being receptive to His leading. God's presence is always with us through his Holy Spirit and He wants us to talk to him. Jeremiah 33:3 says, "Call to me and I will answer you and tell you great and unsearchable things you do not know. There are mysteries of heaven and things we can't understand without God's revelation and wisdom. He is a living God who speaks to His people. One pastor explained that God is a supernatural God. Prayer opens up the dialogue between heaven and earth and invites God into our circumstances, our hearts, and our lives by putting his "super" on our "natural." The Lord is responsive to our call. Psalm 91:15 states, "He will call on me, and I will answer him; I will be with him in trouble, I will deliver him and honor him. God's promise to us continues in the next verse, Psalm 91:16, "With long life I will satisfy him and show him my salvation."

Many prayers are prayed in hospitals, and they are often urgent, passionate prayers. In the ICU, one mom prayed that God would answer her quickly because of her son's critical condition. Another said as she sat next to her child lying in a hospital bed, she felt like her fervent prayers went straight from her lips to God's ears. She knew she needed a miracle and she knew who to go to for it. Many of the people I have worked with have also referenced the importance of their faith and the peace they experience through prayer.

Research studies exploring the benefits of prayer in hospitals cite that benefits of prayer may result in divine intervention, but I think personal experience is the most convincing of all. I talked to a man one time who told me that he had been very ill and in intensive care for some time. He was intubated and sedated and while he was unconscious to those around him, in his slumber and sedation, he felt the prayers of his family and friends "whooshing" past him at a high speed from the earth up to heaven. He felt the movement of those prayers and knew they were making a difference.

God delights in the prayers of his people and maybe especially in the prayers of children.

Recently, our city experienced severe storms and two tornadoes touched down, causing major damage. One of the tornadoes touched down near my sister's house and caused their power to go out. My sister and her husband said the tornado sounded like a freight train as it came through and it was frightening. Their grandchildren were spending the night and they all went to the basement for safety. After the tornado passed, my brother-in-law used the generator to restore power. When the lights came on, two-year-old Mikaela said, "We safe! Thank you, Jesus." She knew that it was Jesus who whooshed in to keep her safe and she thanked Him for it. May we all have the faith to do the same.

Do not be anxious about anything,
but in every situation, by prayer and petition,
with thanksgiving, present your requests to God.
Philippians 4:6

"We safe! Thank you, Jesus."

—Two-year-old Mikaela

8.
Little Bird

One spring morning several years ago, I woke up feeling very anxious. The feelings were intense and unpleasant and I didn't know any specific reason for the cause, but it was an active time with many changes taking place. My husband and I were staying at a rustic cabin for the week.

As I walked from the bedroom to the kitchen to make coffee, some movement from the old screened-in porch caught my attention. I looked closer and saw a scared little bird flying frantically back and forth in the small room, trying to get out. It had come in through a hole in the screen.

I felt the Lord's message in my heart, "That is you."

That simple message quickly reassured me and reminded me that God takes care of the birds and He takes care of me. A blanket of anxiety lifted off of me as I thought about this. I walked out onto the porch and opened the door for the bird to fly free.

Jesus talked to his disciples about birds and flowers and to consider God's care of them. He spoke about how the birds don't worry about provision like food and shelter and neither should we, because God our Father knows our every need. We are even more valuable to Him than the birds.

Our yard has many trees which have attracted a lot of birds, so I bought a bird feeder and began to enjoy their activity and singing even more.

The behavior of the birds showed me their contentment in the moment. It occurred to me that when I focus on my problems and fears, it seems to enlarge them and skews my perception.

In comparison, when I consider "a bird's eye view," it helps to enlarge my understanding by shifting my focus from a limited view to one from a fuller scope. It helps me recall the faithfulness of the Lord and reminds me that our Provider will provide, just as He has done in the past.

The birds and the flowers trust God and so can I.

Consider the ravens: They do not sow or reap, they have no storeroom or barn; yet God feeds them. And how much more valuable you are than birds!
Luke 12:24

"I didn't get scared by the doctor!"

—**A toddler in the ER after her exam**

9.
Feeling Tall

One night when I was working in the ER, I was paged to the rehab (physical rehabilitation) unit. A nurse was waiting for me at the nurses station and explained that a ten-year-old named Nina was confined to a wheelchair. She was worried about her spine surgery the next day. Her hospitalization had been a lengthy one and she needed to have one more back surgery and then she could finally go home.

Before I followed the nurse to the patient's room, she explained that Nina spoke both English and Spanish but was the only English speaking member in her family and would often translate information to her parents and brother.

When I entered the room, Nina was waiting for me expectantly and both of her parents were visiting. She was small for her age and smiled at me shyly when I suggested some activities I had brought for us to do. She and I decided to go to the outdoor play area down the hall.

I had brought a surgery preparation book, a variety of art materials, books, and an assortment of medical supplies for medical play. We explored the outdoor play area for a few minutes but then settled into a space away from the climbing structure that had a tented roof. She and I sat on a blanket on the floor to give

Nina freedom from the wheelchair. We looked at the surgery prep book first and talked about the next day's surgery.

Nina seemed to enjoy herself and was happy about using markers to decorate a cloth hospital doll that was sewn with fabric and filled with stuffing. These cloth hospital dolls were often used as "patients" for medical play. She talked about her family and looked forward to the surgery being over and being able to go home.

I asked Nina about what things had helped her while she was in the hospital. Nina stated that she felt like the character "Madeline" from the *Madeline* books by Ludwig Bemelmans.

She recited:

"I'm Madeline, I'm Madeline,

And though I'm very small,

I'm Madeline, I'm Madeline,

And inside, I'm tall."

She looked at me proudly and smiled.

We cleaned up our things and made our way back to her room. Her parents smiled when they saw her and her nurse commented on how happy she seemed. She wasn't the only one. I walked away smiling and made my way back to the ER feeling taller myself.

Beloved, I pray that you may prosper in all things and be in health, just as your soul prospers.

3 John 1:2

"There's my friend!"
—The greeting of a three-year-old cardiology patient every time she saw me

10.
Agents of the Day

"Ministry Extreme" is how one of the hospital chaplains referred to his pastoral care role. Pastor Jerry and I met while working with some of the same patients, which opened the door for deeper understanding of his ministry.

I asked about how he introduced himself to patients and families. He answered that he introduced himself as part of the hospital team who is someone to talk to about problems.

He said some families didn't know what a chaplain was and others viewed his presence as an indicator of critical news regarding their loved one, though pastoral support was available to anyone.

He explained that although often unknown, pastoral care was available to support staff as well as patients and their families. His experiences talking with staff had been primarily with nurses, who discussed the difficulty of their work. Many felt working with intense and serious situations had a negative impact on both family time and home life.

He said he had less opportunity to work with physicians, though occasionally he had been asked for prayer. One surgeon asked him to pray over his hands prior to a difficult surgery.

He told me about some of the stories that have affected him. One was of a teenager, who, within days of dying had a calm demeanor and who told Pastor Jerry that he was looking forward to seeing Jesus who will greet him on the other side. Another teenager wanted to talk to Pastor Jerry because he had questions about God. As they spoke, the young man explained that since he had been in the hospital, he had been thinking about the Jesus he had learned about in Sunday school as a child. The patient's mom returned to the hospital and when she walked into his room she said, "Something is different about you!" She told her son, "Something has changed!"

He smiled in response and told her he had accepted Jesus in his heart. His mom told him, "I've been praying for you!" At that point, Pastor Jerry left the room for them to spend time together privately but he felt privileged to see that exchange between the mother and son.

Pastor Jerry stated that, not surprisingly, many people blame God for the illness of their child. It's always challenging to see children in pain and suffering, but it's especially difficult for families and others who love that child.

Some people are drawn closer to God during such a crisis, while others struggle with the issue of faith during critical times. Some vary in their reactions because emotions can be strong and changing when circumstances are painful and uncertain.

Pastor Jerry stated he has been grieved by what some church pastors have taught some families in their congregation. Often church families are of great help and comfort, but not always. I told him I had heard many sad stories of teenagers who attempted suicide being told they would go to hell and situations of parents being told their sin caused their child's illness. How tragic for people in pain to experience judgment and alienation from the same people who could have been showing them kindness and support. It's also sad for God, who is a God of love and comfort, to be so misrepresented.

We talked about how we had witnessed such hard things through our work and I acknowledged that his role was an extremely challenging one. Pastor Jerry answered, "We are the agents of the day, doing what we can one day at a time; one moment at a time." He continued, "The more we discipline ourselves, the more the Holy Spirit can use us."

We talked about the ER and some of the tragic situations encountered there, including traumas and deaths. He talked about how unpredictable outcomes were and how there was no reassurance for families that things would work out well.

When a death did occur in the ER, a room was closed for privacy so that families could stay and say goodbye to their loved one. Pastor Jerry said in these situations, when the parents were ready to go home, he would walk them to the door and pray with them before they left.

Pastor Jerry stated that with sadness comes an appreciation for life. He explained that he owned some land, and had previously enjoyed hunting, but now it is a sport he no longer participated in. The last time he went hunting, he aimed at a deer ahead of him. The deer looked up and Pastor Jerry realized he couldn't shoot. It was just something he couldn't enjoy anymore.

During one of our conversations, Pastor Jerry told me about how he had become a chaplain. He had been a businessman who enjoyed his work and was married with two children. Then one night he had a vivid dream and when he woke up, he felt certain the Lord was leading him to change careers and return to school to become a chaplain. He followed through with the instructions of that dream.

God had seen Pastor Jerry's teachable heart and called him into "Ministry Extreme."

Comfort, comfort my people, says your God.
Isaiah 40:1

"The more we can discipline ourselves, the more the Holy Spirit can use us."

—A hospital chaplain

11.
Elevator Going Up

One of my earliest experiences working with a patient in heart failure was with a five-year-old boy, Kevin. He was small for his age and tired easily, although he had a great imagination and loved to play.

He liked going to the playroom and was enthusiastic about any activity, but his favorite activities were medical play and playing with shaving cream.

Sometimes play sessions were held in his room, if he was low on energy or if we were limited on time. Kevin's mom stayed with him much of the time. His dad and brother visited in the evenings and brought him his favorite toys from home during his lengthy hospitalization.

Kevin missed his two dogs at home but he had a favorite stuffed animal, a bunny which accompanied him almost everywhere he went. As a five-year-old learning to read, Kevin decided the words sewn on the bunny's tag was his name. The bunny's name was, "Made in China" which he pronounced in a sing-song voice.

After diagnostic testing, it was determined that Kevin needed a heart transplant. One day in his room during medical play, he sat in bed and busily performed "heart surgery" on a hospital doll.

I sat on a chair next to his bed and his mom, Diane, sat across the room and read a book.

A few minutes later, a man entered the room and Diane got up to greet him. She introduced me to her friend as the pastor of their church. She seemed happy to see him and briefly interrupted Kevin's play, asking him to say "hello" before she and the pastor stood and talked.

I offered to stay with Kevin so they could leave the room and talk privately but they politely declined my offer.

My attention was focused on Kevin, but the small room didn't allow for private conversations. The pastor asked Diane how she was doing and asked questions pertaining to the family's needs.

Diane answered, "This is just something we need to go through. Kevin will be fine; I know it. God is with us, but it's just something we need to go through."

I quickly glanced her way to assess her demeanor which was one of calmness and strength. They spoke a little longer and Diane thanked him for the church's support and provision, including prayer.

Not long after, Kevin received a heart transplant, recovered well, and was able to be discharged. The entire staff grew fond of this family and celebrated when Kevin and "Made in China" were able to go home again.

Later, after a follow-up appointment in the cardiology clinic, Diane asked the staff to page me. Kevin had drawn me a picture that he wanted to give me.

We had a short but very good visit. I commented on how much he had grown and Diane happily agreed. She said his energy level had improved tremendously and he could play and not tire so easily.

As our visit came to an end, we walked down the hall together. Kevin walked ahead of us and then stopped suddenly and pushed an imaginary button. I looked at Diane and she explained that he was pretending to wait for an elevator.

We both started laughing and Diane said that even his imagination was much more active than before his surgery.

Kevin's elevator was pretend; but his bright personality was for real.

"For I know the plans I have for you," declares the LORD, "plans to prosper you and not to harm you, plans to give you hope and a future."
Jeremiah 29:11

"My friend is an OR (operating room) nurse. Before Mathew's heart transplant, she held his heart in her hands and prayed over it."

—A cardiology nurse

12.
A Library of Memories

One day I was out running errands wearing a sweatshirt with the hospital's name and logo on it. I stopped by the library to pick up some books and the librarian smiled at me as I approached her desk. As she checked out my books, she asked me if I worked at children's hospital and what I did there.

I explained I was a child life specialist and she went on to tell me that her granddaughter was in the NICU (Neonatal Intensive Care Unit) for four months because of a rare and complex medical condition. The baby's condition was diagnosed in utero and her birth was induced much earlier than her expected due date. She was now ten months old and small for her age, but thriving.

I could tell the grandmother wanted to say more but a man approached the desk with several books in hand to check out, bringing our conversation to a close. I told her that we see a lot of miracles there and she smiled and verbalized her agreement.

As I said goodbye and started to walk away, she called out, "We love you guys!" It choked me up. People want to tell their story. Connections are made both inside and outside of the hospital due to life events that happen there.

Significant moments in a loved ones life transpire in a hospital setting, where faith and hope is often tested and becomes a part of our own life story. We all have a library of experiences which influence and shape us as the message of our lives are being written one day at a time.

Your eyes saw my unformed body; all the days ordained for me were written in your book before one of them came to be.
Psalm 139:16

"This is a really good hospital."
"Except for the lab!"

—A conversation between a mom and daughter talking to Grandpa as they walked down the corridor in the direction of the outpatient lab where blood draws were taken

13.
Angels on Call

"Tell Shannon who was with you in the operating room," Mindy's mom said to her. I arrived to see seven-year-old Mindy after surgery, while nurses were getting her settled in the CTICU (Cardiothoracic Intensive Care Unit). I had known Mindy and her parents for years. She was a very sick three-year-old when I met her. Heart and kidney problems had caused many hospitalizations. Mindy looked at me and answered, "Susie (her doll), the angel that came to my room to meet me, Jesus, and thousands and thousands of angels."

I arrived to see her after surgery while nurses were getting her settled in the CTICU (Cardiothoracic Intensive Care Unit). I had known Mindy and her parents for years. She was a very sick three-year-old when I met her. Heart and kidney problems had caused many hospitalizations.

At five, she had to start dialysis treatments three times a week as an outpatient which was really hard for all of them, especially since they lived three hours away and Mindy's mom didn't drive. Then came a call one day informing them they had found a "match" for Mindy to receive a new kidney. They were instructed to come to the hospital immediately.

Her parents and I talked quietly at her bedside as she slept. They told me that two weeks prior, Mindy woke them up one night and told them about an angel who visited her bedroom to meet her. She hadn't been afraid.

That same angel was at her side in the operating room, too, and told her to listen to everything Jesus told her to do. She said the operating room was filled with thousands and thousands of angels.

Mindy's parents were greatly relieved when the surgery was over but they were physically and emotionally exhausted. I suggested they get some sleep in one of the parent sleep rooms and offered to sit with Mindy for a bit while she slept. I reminded them of the capable staff and reassured them that staff would wake them up if there was any need for it.

That night in the CTICU with Mindy stands out from the others. Mindy had encountered holiness and I felt a force field of loving energy surrounding her and filling the room.

When it was time to go, it was hard to leave the strong presence of God but I knew Mindy was in good hands.

For he will command his angels concerning you to guard you in all your ways.
Psalm 91:11

"Is this for real?"

—A seven-year-old in the ER after she was struck by a car

14.
Merry & Bright

When I began in the hospital, I wasn't especially excited about working weekends and holidays. Most therapists and specialists weren't required to, and most received higher salaries than child life specialists, but experience can change minds and it certainly changed mine.

The Christmas season is a busy time of year for child life staff who manage many donations and special events, in addition to maintaining their clinical workload. Despite the extra demands on both time and energy, it soon became one of my favorite times of the year to work. The hospital was always decorated both inside and out. ER staff had an annual door decorating contest which transformed the many exam rooms into festive works of art. Nursing stations and patient rooms were decorated with small Christmas trees, lights, and children's artwork. There was a level of energy and excitement in the air unlike any other time of the year.

The night I met Santa was a memorable one. He and Mrs. Claus had spent many Christmas Eves visiting patients and families in the hospital, going room to room with staff, to visit and encourage those who wanted some holiday cheer. When we reached the cardiology unit, Santa hesitated and quietly told me that he and his wife made a decision a long time ago to spend every Christmas Eve at the hospital instead of with their own children and grandchildren because they know what it was like to be in the hospital with a sick child. Their youngest son had required frequent hospitalizations and multiple surgeries due to congenital heart problems. He had not lived to adulthood but probably would have if the medical advances available now had been available then. They both spoke about how lonely it was in the hospital being isolated from home and all that is familiar. Mrs. Claus said they could never forget how frightening it was to have a sick child and to watch them undergo all that is required of them physically and emotionally. They mentioned the kindness of the staff and connection with the other families they came to know while at the hospital. A moment of quiet sadness settled on the three of us as I took in what they had just shared with me. Then we walked down the hall to the next hospital room. I handed Santa a gift for the baby in the room and he entered, full of charisma once again with his wife close behind. He spoke some words of comfort to the baby's worried mom, squeezing her arm fondly before turning to leave. They were agents of love and that mom's gratitude was obvious.

We continued through the hospital and walked over to another unit. More Christmas surprises were yet to come. We went from room to room, me handing Santa a gift for the age of each patient in the room. We came to the room of a teenager, a seventeen-year-old I knew from multiple admissions through the ER because of severe pain brought on by sickle cell anemia. For reasons I don't remember, he was usually brought to the ER by his mom or by squad and left alone. Whenever that occurred, ER staff paged me to sit with him and keep him company or to check in on him frequently if I was too busy to stay. Sometimes he requested that I rub his back to help alleviate the pain and at other times, he wanted only my quiet presence. I always followed his lead. After receiving pain medicine, we would dim the lights so he could try to rest until he was admitted and taken upstairs to a room. Every time I had ever seen him, he was in excruciating pain. But on this Christmas Eve, he was sitting up in bed with his mom sitting on a nearby couch. He smiled the absolute biggest smile when Santa and Mrs. Claus walked into his room and handed him his present. That was my favorite Christmas present that year: seeing his face light up with joy and not a trace of pain in his eyes.

Another favorite Christmas memory was a few years later on one December evening. There was a holiday party scheduled with activities planned and a visit from Santa and Mrs. Claus. There wasn't a music group available to cover the event so my brother, Mike, and his friend, Chris, both musicians in college at the time, volunteered to come play Christmas music. Both played several instruments but that evening Mike played an upright bass and Chris accompanied with a tenor saxophone.

A variety of donations came pouring in earlier that day, including a large donation of adult-sized Sombrero hats which were too big for the kids. We handed them out to parents and staff and Mike and Chris decided to wear them while they played their music, which added to the festive mood. The event was a huge success and Santa and Mrs. Claus expressed how much they enjoyed the music and evening, too.

After the party was over and patients had been escorted back to their rooms, I suggested Mike and Chris help themselves to the submarine sandwiches which had been ordered for staff and volunteers working that evening. The staff and I thanked them for performing and they said they enjoyed it, but that it was hard for them to see so many sick kids with IV's, bandages, and in wheelchairs.

I apologized it wasn't a paid performance for them as they often had paid engagements around town, but my brother answered that it was their pleasure to participate and even if they had been paid, they probably would have used the money to buy sandwiches and Sombreros, so it worked out well for them.

Santa and Mrs. Claus continued their hospital tradition for almost thirty years before his oldest son and his wife took over the tradition and continued on. I have great appreciation for those who give of themselves through working, volunteering, and donating to bring glimmers of what is Merry and Bright to others. The Spirit of Christmas is a Spirit of Love; which is seen, felt, and known from deep within us.

And now these three remain: faith, hope and love. But the greatest of these is love.
1 Corinthians 13:13

"Hospitalizations are deeply transformative. I would add that despite the hardship, these experiences can result in tremendous personal, emotional, and spiritual growth."

—A father of a hospitalized child

15. Champagne Friends

A favorite room in my home is a sunroom filled with plants, which I've collected throughout the years. Among the plants is a large twenty-year old avocado tree started from seed by a friend, Eric.

My husband, Ed, and I were introduced to Eric and his wife, Trish, many years ago by a mutual acquaintance who arranged a dinner because she thought we should know one another. That night was the beginning of a beautiful friendship between the four of us.

From the start, they felt more like family to us than just friends. We didn't see each other often, we lived across town in different communities, but when we did, it was often to celebrate birthdays and holidays.

One New Year's Eve, Eric and Trish invited us to spend the night at their home so we could toast with champagne and continue the cooking and visiting into New Year's Day together. Ed and Eric both loved to cook and that night, they prepared a gourmet dinner for Trish and I, wearing chef hats and coats. It's one of the many vivid memories I have of the four of us. There was always easy laughter between us but we were able to talk about weightier topics, too.

After our daughter, Audrey, was born, they were the only friends we included in her baptism ceremony besides family. Six months later, they had a daughter of their own, Elayna, giving us more to celebrate.

As Audrey and Elayna were growing up, they were always happy to see one another. Both girls were creative and artistic by nature. They also played with our dogs and Elayna often reminded her hesitant dad of reasons they should get a dog. Trish wanted one, too. Eric said he liked dogs but not the mess they made. When Elayna was still asking for a dog years later, he agreed and they adopted an adult dog named Bella from the shelter. Bella had been returned to the shelter by two previous owners, but she was Elayna's choice. Bella the Beagle found her forever home. Trish said the previous owners returned her to the shelter because they must have sensed that it wasn't the right fit as a family and Bella was only visiting them until she found her true family. Eric liked the dog right away and she liked him. Eric told Trish he couldn't explain it but there was something about Bella that felt familiar and she somehow reminded Eric of his brother who had become ill and passed away years prior.

Late one night, Eric experienced sudden chest pain and Trish called the emergency squad. He was admitted to the ICU (Intensive Care Unit) where he remained under heavy sedation. His outcome was uncertain. Slowly, he showed signs of improvement. When he started feeling better and was able to talk, Eric told Trish that his brother who had passed away years prior had visited him in the ICU.

Eric miraculously returned home where he rested and worked on building strength for heart surgery that was to be performed at a hospital out of town. When the time came, the surgery and recovery went well and a discharge date was determined.

On the morning of Eric's anticipated discharge day, Trish woke up to a message from Eric who had texted in the middle of the night a Happy Mother's Day message. Trish was confused because Mother's Day was several days away and Eric would be home by then. She texted him and asked him to call her when he woke up.

When Eric called, he told Trish he had had a dream that he forgot to wish her a Happy Mother's Day, which he wouldn't want to do, so he texted her in the middle of the night. They discussed their plans for the day and the anticipated discharge time that evening.

Trish's neighbor, knowing how tired Trish was from driving back and forth between cities to care for her husband and daughter, offered to drive and accompany her to the hospital. When they were halfway there, Trish received an urgent call from the hospital advising her to come right away. She explained she was on her way and would be there shortly.

She arrived at the hospital to the heartbreaking news that Eric had passed away. Peacefully and unexpectedly, he had gone to his heavenly home with his brother and wouldn't be home for Mother's Day after all. But before he died, he obeyed the prompting of his dream and honored his wife with a Happy Mother's Day message.

Meanwhile, Elayna, who was at home, felt a precise moment of spiritual shift and a sorrowful awareness when her dad's spirit had left this world for the next. Even before the surgery she had sadly sensed that her dad wouldn't be coming back home.

Naturally, the time that followed was a time of grief, mourning, and adjustment with many unanswered questions and much to do. One day, Trish and a friend were sorting through Eric's things, with Bella at their side. Bella rolled over on her back requesting a belly rub. As Trish rubbed her belly, her friend noticed a white marking in the shape of a cross on Bella's belly, yet another heavenly sign.

Life is full of new beginnings for no two days are alike. In the rhythm of life, some seasons change gradually and some change suddenly, but in the midst of our routines and busy schedules, we and our friends chose to make time to celebrate our blessings and everyday moments. All along the way, we created memories during dinners and football games, Fourth of July picnics and fireworks.

God tells such beautiful stories through our everyday lives. I appreciate the history our two families have shared, for our yesterdays are the foundation for our tomorrows, and yesterday's prayers are being realized in our today.

Today, our beautiful and creative daughters are both in college with futures full of promise. Ed and I are fulfilling our dream of designing and building a home and Trish has found new love, purpose, and opportunities.

Eric wouldn't have wanted Trish to be alone and she credits him in guiding her to meeting one of his college friends who is a good man with a fun personality. And Bella the Beagle loves her new dad.

The last time we had Trish and John over for dinner, Trish and I had time to talk privately in the kitchen. Tracing the color and movement of the grain in my granite countertop with her finger, she said, "Life is a flow, it's movement, it's ever changing. It's not what happens to you; it's what you do with it."

And in the flow of life, we learned to take notice in the gifts of today, for they are the memories of tomorrow.

Your eyes saw my unformed body; all the days ordained for me were written in your book before one of them came to be.
Psalm 139:16

> "Life is a flow, it's movement, it's ever changing. It's not what happens to you; it's what you do with it."
>
> —My friend, Trish

16.
X-Ray Vision

We see a lot of tears at the hospital, but we see a lot of laughter, too.

One ten-year-old boy liked to greet the hospital staff after his heart surgery by wearing a fake mustache with an adhesive backing. He had a selection of sizes and styles and he laughed as hard as we did every time we came into his room.

Another patient I worked with who had a sunny disposition was a toddler who was briefly hospitalized for observation. I talked with her mom and aunt while she played happily in her crib. Her mom explained that her toddler was a twin and had several older brothers and sisters. She was used to getting lots of attention and had never been away from them before but was adjusting well.

She told me that they had just returned from the radiology department. She stated that while in the waiting area, they saw a fifteen-year-old also waiting for x-rays. He had been wheeled to the radiology department in his bed and had many tubes and wires attached to him. She said that she had a hard time looking at him because he looked so sick and so sad. He rested in bed with his eyes closed until her daughter called out, "CHOO!," in his direction, trying to get his attention.

"CHOO!," she called out again with her eyes fixed on him. He slowly opened his eyes and turned his head in her direction to find her staring straight at him expectantly. He smiled back at her.

The teen's mom commented that it was the first time he had smiled in a week. The toddler's mom replied that pretending to sneeze to make her siblings laugh was one of her daughter's newer tricks.

The mom and aunt told me of their concern for the teenager and his mom. They didn't know what floor he was on or what was wrong with him but they felt terrible for them. They said it was sad to see him so sick and his mom so worried.

Connection and compassion among strangers is common in the hospital. It doesn't take X-ray vision to see when someone is in pain. A kind word or a supportive glance can communicate encouragement in much needed situations. Sometimes it can be as simple as a fake sneeze and a smile between a toddler and a teen.

**A cheerful heart is good medicine,
but a crushed spirit dries up the bones.**
Proverbs 17:22

"Is it going to hurt?"

—A frequent question by patients of all ages

17.
Holy Ground

There was a small chapel at the hospital which was located off the main lobby. Services were held in observance of holy days for different faiths. Bibles and other religious materials were available for people to use.

An annual service was held for the hospital staff called, "The Blessing of the Hands." God's work is often performed through human hands. He establishes the work of our hands to heal, hold, and to provide comfort and care. It is a short ceremony because of busy schedules, but a very meaningful one. I was able to attend a few of these services.

Memorial services for patients after a death are commonly held outside the hospital by the family, but one of the families we worked with requested a separate memorial for all the healthcare workers that had taken care of their son. They saw how much we cared about their family and wanted to include us and thank us because he spent more time in the hospital than he did at home. They appreciated the time they did have together.

He had been so sick after he was born because of complex heart issues that some of his surgeries had to be performed in the CTICU (Cardiothoracic Intensive Care Unit) because he was not medically stable enough to be transferred to the operating room.

Though always hopeful, neither parents nor staff thought he would ever leave the CTICU but he started to show improvement and his personality began to emerge.

When he was six-months-old, he was able to be transferred to the cardiology unit. He progressed medically, socially, and developmentally and he enjoyed the company and attention of his family and all the medical staff. Nurses jokingly fought over who would get to be his assigned nurse.

It was with great excitement when he was finally able to go home. He did well at his follow-up cardiology appointments but a few months after he was home, he unexpectedly passed away.

On the day of the memorial, the Chaplain, Father Terrance, and both parents spoke and read scripture. Father Terrance told us that everyone thinks that death is the worst thing that can happen to a child, but it's not. He said the greatest need that children have is to be loved and cared for. The worst thing is for children and people to question why they are here on earth and to wonder if they matter.

Next came an invitation for others to share memories or comments if they chose. The small room was filled with tearful moments mixed with laughter as stories of this sweet child were told.

Afterwards, the chaplain invited everyone to come up front and circle around the altar for the Lord's Prayer. We held hands and prayed in unison. It was incredibly powerful.

We ended by sharing words of peace with one another and we took turns speaking to the family. I hugged them and thanked them for giving us the chance to say goodbye and they again expressed how much we all meant to them.

Shannon Alford

As others engaged in conversation around us, I had a moment alone with Father Terrance. I knew he was greatly respected by families and staff but my previous interactions with him had been limited to hallways or the nurse's station.

I commented on how the chapel is close to the busy hospital lobby yet the atmosphere felt entirely different within its walls than outside them. God's presence was felt in the chapel and he smiled and said, "This place is holy, this is holy ground." Then he referenced the account of Moses standing on holy ground in the book of Exodus.

Next he told me a story. During his studies, he read of a hospital chaplain that came across a crying and grieving woman. He told her that he wished there was something that he could do to help her but there wasn't. Instead, he would take her to someone who could and he walked her to the chapel.

God lifts our burdens. He knows how hard this life can be for us sometimes and He is with us to help us. He warns us that in this world we will have trouble, but to take heart! Jesus has overcome the world.

> **"I have told you these things, so that in me you may have peace. In this world you will have trouble. But take heart! I have overcome the world."**
> *John 16:33*

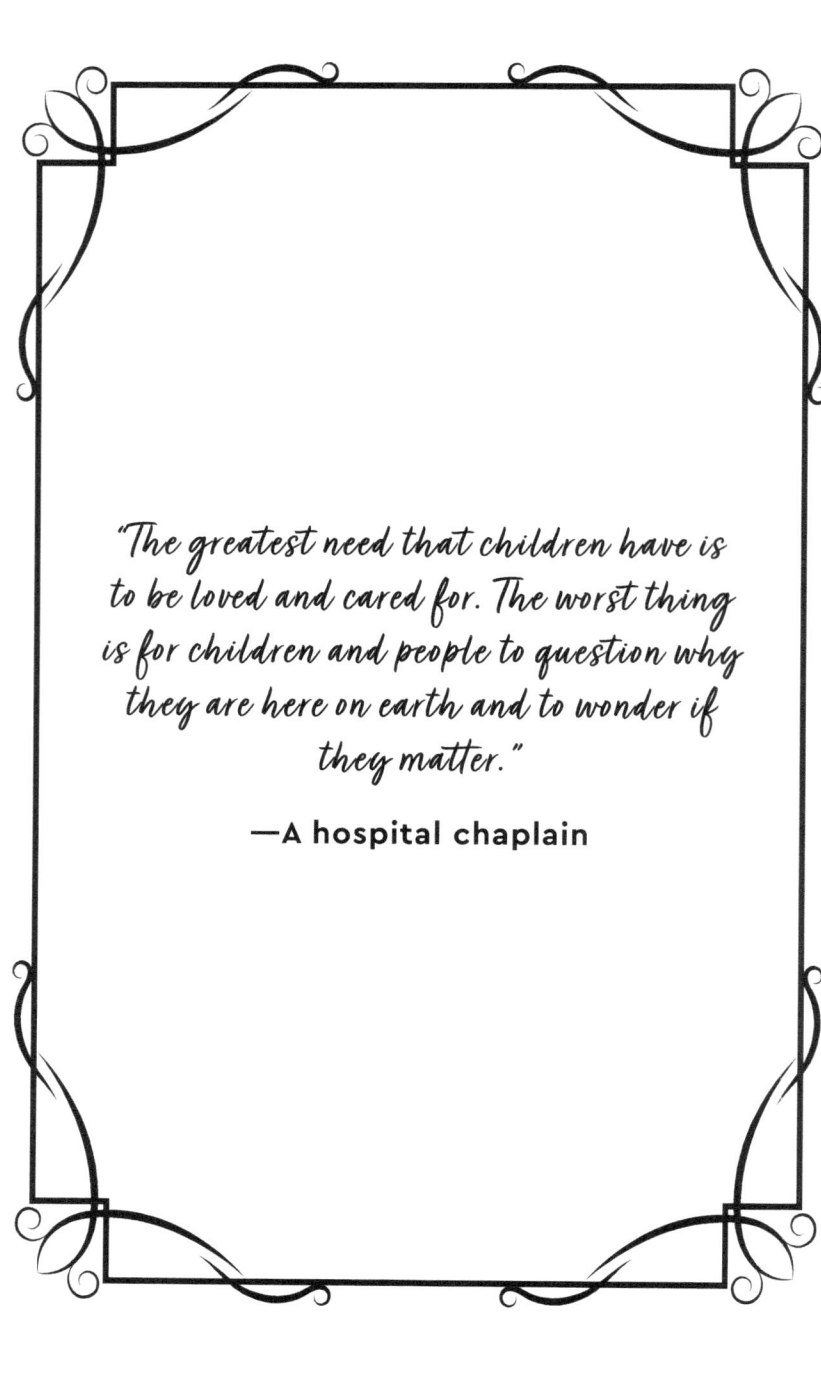

"The greatest need that children have is to be loved and cared for. The worst thing is for children and people to question why they are here on earth and to wonder if they matter."

—A hospital chaplain

18.
Shining Stars

One of the ways child life specialists promote normal development and socialization for patients during a child's hospital stay is through supervised and scheduled events as well as through interaction in activity groups. Some of the activity groups target an age specific population, while other activity groups include all ages, such as bingo and dog visits. Activity groups allow a time of normalcy for children and adolescents to be with peers along with the freedom to express themselves creatively. It provides an opportunity for independence, at least for a short time, without the focus on illness and medical intervention.

I met Jeremy while I was supervising a teen group at the hospital. He was nineteen years old and experienced frequent and long hospitalizations due to a diagnosis of Cystic Fibrosis.

As I was introducing activity options, he was moving slowly and commented on how old he felt. A well-meaning volunteer who was assisting with the activity group that day, overheard his comment to me and interjected that he was too young to feel that way and to "just wait" until he was as old as she was.

The woman meant no harm but I inwardly cringed at her comment. Most likely, he will not live to be past the age of retirement as she was. Regardless of his age, no one can fathom his challenges from battling such a disease.

I was glad to see him again when he returned for an activity group on another day in which he and two teenage girls attended. He was the first to arrive and he helped me set out materials.

As we were finishing setting up, one teenager walked into the room to join us. A few minutes later, a nurse arrived pushing a patient in a wheelchair who was deaf. The nurse explained that she really enjoyed arts and craft activities, although the teenager looked hesitant and unsure about being there.

As the nurse and I created more space for the wheelchair at the activity table, Jeremy started signing to her. She visibly relaxed and smiled in response. I looked at him with surprise and he told me he knew sign language. Group that day was fun and interactive with the three teenagers.

After the group ended that day and nurses helped the girls return to their individual rooms on different floors, I walked Jeremy to his room which was located down the hall. I thanked him for his assistance in making the shy teenager feel so comfortable.

Jeremy's room was a larger corner room at the end of the hallway with big windows on two sides. He told me it was his favorite room because of the view. The nurses, if they could, always tried to give him this room whenever he was hospitalized.

There was a Bible on the table next to his bed. He noticed that I had glanced at it and told me that he liked to look at the stars through the windows at night because it is when he feels closest to God.

Our God knows us and loves us. One of the ways He speaks to us is through the beauty of His Creation.

I am grateful that Jeremy felt close to God and that he knew he was not alone. His body was frail but his faith was radiant.

Shannon Alford

Those who are wise will shine like the brightness of the heavens, and those who lead many to righteousness, like the stars for ever and ever.

Daniel 12:3

"The doctors aren't God, but God is everywhere here."

—A patient's grandmother

19.
The Magic of Music

Child life specialists and music therapists work closely together. Jennifer was the music therapist I worked with most frequently and a friendship naturally grew between us.

Music therapists provided individual and group sessions. Children naturally love music and music therapy is deemed beneficial for all ages.

The mother of a teenager in PICU (Pediatric Intensive Care Unit) told Jennifer that her job was a beautiful ministry and how her son seemed soothed and not agitated when she played her guitar and sang for him. The mom said she looked forward to the music, too, during the long days in intensive care while waiting for her son to become well enough to be transferred to a medical floor.

Jennifer told me that she had never considered her profession as a ministry before. I see the peace, comfort, and joy she and her profession bring to patients and their families, and I have always considered it a ministry.

One day when I was talking to a mom of a one-year-old, she explained that her son was recently adopted and was having a rough time medically during this hospital stay. She told me a nurse had tried unsuccessfully to start an IV (intravenous) so the IV team had been called and was expected to arrive shortly.

I paged Jennifer and she was able to adjust her schedule to make him a priority. He sat on his mom's lap and watched Jennifer with interest when she got out her guitar. He seemed to enjoy the music and had the sweetest look on his face.

I sat near her and made hand motions to the songs she played like "Twinkle Twinkle Little Star" and "The Itsy Bitsy Spider." He watched both of us and stared at me expectantly, even when she sang songs with no known hand movements, so I improvised the best I could.

As the session came near an end, the mom thanked Jennifer for the visit and told her that this was the happiest her son had been since they arrived at the hospital. Jennifer asked if there were any songs she didn't sing that they would like to hear and the mom answered that a favorite of theirs is "Jesus loves me."

As Jennifer began to sing, I choked back tears and laughter at the same time. I was moved by how beautiful her voice and guitar sounded together and amused at the one-year-old staring at me to perform accompanying hand gestures that I started to make up.

The IV team arrived as we were leaving. We spoke with them briefly and they thanked us for visiting their little patient who had undergone some difficult experiences. I later learned that the IV placement had been successful.

On the day I met this cute little guy, he was having a difficult time. The early months of his childhood had gotten off to a rough start but he was adopted by a family who loved him and would raise him well.

God sets the lonely in families,
Psalm 68:6

> *"Chris is the baby whisperer. He can calm babies down better than anyone."*
>
> —One cardiology nurse about another

20.
Here to Help

Memories of my cousin, John, have come to mind as the anniversary of his passing from this world to the next approaches. Illness may have taken a toll on his body, but his spirit and purpose remained strong all of his days. His influence lives on.

John was someone people liked to be around. He was a natural leader and teacher. His strengths developed further through his service as a soldier, EMT (emergency medical technician) instructor, and fire chief. He used his scope of influence well, caring for the people around him. What a beautiful legacy to leave.

When he was an EMT instructor, he taught his students that the first thing to do when arriving on the scene of an accident is to look the patient in the eye and tell them, "We're here to help." That exemplifies how he lived his life and brought such purpose to it.

John had the ability to bring calm, direction, and often humor to serious situations and I experienced that with him when we were teenagers. My aunt and uncle had invited me on their family vacation to Florida to stay on a houseboat, to join my three cousins and them on their family vacation. We were close in age, with John being the youngest.

On the first day, John suggested he and I use the canoe and explore the area. Being from the midwest, we grew up around lakes but not oceans, and this was our first trip to Florida.

John and I hadn't been canoeing very long when my oar hit something solid instead of gliding through the water. Looking down, I saw a massive fishlike monster swimming directly under our canoe and scenes from the movie "Jaws" flashed in my mind. I thought our small boat would be captized and glanced back at John nervously as I tried to brace myself for whatever happened next.

John cautiously watched the huge creature moving slowly underneath our boat and calmly said something funny like he wasn't hoping to die on our first day of vacation. He also suggested we turn around and paddle back to the houseboat. Later that day, John and I learned that we had seen a manatee, which is a gentle and social marine mammal, and we had never been in actual danger. John's leadership and calm demeanor helped me then and helped him later succeed in his professional positions, too.

Thinking back on those moments- in the space between fear and safety, while facing the unknown, is something all will experience at some point in life. We all go through times of trouble. During times like these, look for the "helpers" around you.

One of my cousin's goals was to become a nurse like his mom. When his daughters grew older, he retired as a fire chief and enrolled in nursing school. The other students, who were young classmates, struggled with the course load so John organized a study group to review and learn together, sharing also from his experiences. They met regularly until health issues unexpectedly occurred and John was home in heaven before they officially became RN's (registered nurses). But on graduation day, there was an empty chair with John's name on it to honor him as part of their class and they dedicated the ceremony to him. Love lives on.

One cousin told me she and her sisters all woke up in the middle of the night when they felt a spiritual shift of his soul leaving this world. They had perceived the sad news before they received a call from the hospital.

John and my brother, Mike, had a close friendship. They were close in age and had a lot of common interests. John's loss was hard on my brother and apparently John knew it, too, because one night in my brother's dream, John visited Mike to tell him that he is well and everything is okay. John told him there was no need to worry. My brother said John seemed really happy in the dream and they met on a grassy area, though he sensed they were near a large body of water. My cousin was a boater and had sailed all his life with his dad exploring the Great Lakes.

Even from heaven, John was a caretaker and an encourager intervening to help.

**For we are God's handiwork,
created in Christ Jesus to do good works,
which God prepared in advance for us to do.**
Ephesians 2:10

"I don't know how you do it."

"I have to. Someone needs to and if I didn't, more kids would go Home home, instead of just home." (the nurse gestured by pointing her finger up to Heaven)

"I was in the ER with my daughter not long ago and it was tough. I'd rather be a nurse helping other people."

—A conversation between a parent and a cardiology nurse

21.
Drawn to Healing

Teenage boys were the population which took the most time and respectful persistence for me to develop a rapport. Wyatt was one such patient. I met him briefly during one short hospital stay, but that was soon followed by a lengthy hospitalization. He had stopped taking his heart medication which sent him into heart failure and resulted in him being a candidate for a heart transplant. He was one of many children and his family lived out of town. His mom had serious health issues and his dad worked a lot of hours, but he was well-loved and his family visited him when they could, which was primarily on the weekends. His older brother, out of high school and working, was able to visit the most and sometimes spent the night with him in his room.

Almost daily, I made my way to Wyatt's room to suggest activities and attempt to connect with him. Finally, frustration and boredom led him to accept my offer, and we began to meet regularly in the family room located on the unit which more closely resembled a home environment than a hospital. One day, a nurse informed me that Wyatt was depressed most of the time, but he looked forward to his scheduled child life time. She stated that about a half hour before my arrival, he would go to the family room and wait expectantly. He and I both enjoyed our time together. I came to know his mischievous ways and his great sense of humor while we participated in creative activities and projects. Sometimes the music therapist joined us, playing guitar and singing for us, and taking our requests for songs.

It was also through Wyatt that a friendship developed. Tami was one of the hospital school teachers and Wyatt was her student. Tami and I began to sometimes coordinate our schedules so we could play board games together which focused on learning but also increased the fun by having more participants. Nurses and patient care assistants were always willing to join in when their schedules allowed. Wyatt's wait for a heart transplant was long because his blood type was harder to match, but eventually he had his surgery, recovered, and was able to go home.

During his recovery, Tami and Wyatt worked together on a PowerPoint presentation about his heart problems and transplant. He did a great job and received school credit for his project. A few days after Wyatt was discharged, the unit clerk glanced into his empty room while walking down the hall and said, "I miss him." She voiced what others and I had been thinking, even though we were happy he was finally home with his family. He had resided at the hospital for so long, it appeared he seemed to view his room as his own apartment and, as staff, we had grown accustomed to his residency.

Another young man I enjoyed working with was seventeen-year-old Anthony. He had a history of heart problems and was hospitalized after a stroke. I met him early in my career before hospital renovations were completed. The patient rooms were small and semi-private, lacking the privacy and comfort later available with new facilities. There also wasn't the technology and entertainment available then that there is today.

Anthony became discouraged because of his illness and his separation from his family and friends. He had a lot of concerns about his future, especially since there was uncertainty regarding the extent of damage caused by the stroke. Both his parents worked and he didn't have any brothers or sisters. His mom occasionally visited during the day but usually both parents visited in the evening. After several attempts to engage Anthony in individual and group activities, he became more receptive and soon became interested in joining me on a project. He was creative and liked to draw. He was able to express some of the feelings he was experiencing through his art and while he was initially hesitant to share his artwork, he became more open about it and we encouraged him to hang it on the walls. It gave Wyatt a sense of control and pride and it also helped us gain insight as to what he was thinking. His health, mood, and energy increased.

One day I went to Anthony's room and met his dad for the first and only time. Anthony was drawing in bed. After I introduced myself to Anthony's dad, he asked to speak to me out in the hall. His request surprised me, but I followed him down the hall to an empty corridor. He looked me straight in the eyes and said, "You were sent here by God." I was at a loss for words. He repeated again, "You were sent here by God. I have been praying for my son and it is answered prayer to see him excited about something and thinking about his future again. Thank you."

Sometime later, I ran into Wyatt when I stopped by the cardiology clinic to deliver donations and he was there for a clinic appointment. He smiled and was talkative with all of us. It was great to see him happy and healthy, just as I hoped he would be.

Spiritual Ink

Pour out your heart like water in the presence of the Lord. Lift up your hands to him for the lives of your children.
Lamentations 2:19

"I know what you mean, jellybean."

—A conversation between two patients having a difficult day

22.
Good Medicine

The connection between dogs and people is a strong one. The use of therapy and facility dogs within the hospital setting promotes healing components of joy, comfort, and therapeutic support.

Regularly scheduled visits with therapy dogs and their volunteer owners allow children and adults the opportunity to pet and interact with the visiting dog. The children like to ask the volunteers questions about their pet and the pet owners have expressed how much their dogs like the attention they receive during the hospital visits. They have said that their dogs seem to know when it is a visitation day even before the car ride because of the routine grooming involved in the preparation including a bath and wearing a special bandana.

I remember one day a ten-year-old boy was being wheeled down the hall in a wheelchair by a staff member. His parents followed behind them. The nurse and I stood nearby discussing which patients were able to leave the unit to attend the event. The nurse suggested the patient before us might want to visit a dog and we walked towards them together to ask. The patient responded with an enthusiastic "yes," but his mom followed up with a "no," stating that he had just come from surgery and was going back to his room to rest. The boy insisted he wanted to visit the dog and asked for the nurse's permission to go, looking to her for help to overrule his mom. The nurse offered reassurance that he was fine to go if he wanted to so the mom agreed. Watching that family that afternoon, you would have never guessed this child had been in the operating room hours earlier. The boy looked happy and his parents looked more relaxed. The dog visit was good for all of them.

A friend of mine had worked with two toddlers during their extended hospitalizations and she described the look on these children's faces when their parents brought them together in their strollers to a dog visit. They had been in the hospital for so long that it was the first time either of them had ever seen a dog. They squealed with delight, kicking their feet, looking at one another and then back at the dog again in wonder. She said their joy is something she will never forget.

The hospital also had facility dogs which are professionally trained to work in a clinical setting with their designated handler. One of the dogs, Murphy, was a black lab who participated with therapists in the rehabilitation program. Murphy lived with his owner, Lindsey, and her family. I met with Lindsey to learn more about how Murphy assists therapists and helps patients. As Lindsey and I talked, he slept on his rug in the corner of her office.

Lindsey told me Murphy has his own schedule which she posts outside her office door. Different therapists on the rehab team incorporate him into their therapies in helping children reach specific goals. Children naturally respond more enthusiastically to a dog than simply another adult asking them to perform a difficult and painful task.

Lindsey said Murphy loves to go to work with her each day. He sleeps on his rug when his schedule is free. She noticed that he appeared depressed when she was on maternity leave and then regained his typical enthusiasm once she returned to work. Her family has also enjoyed him as their family dog, although at times her children object that he gets to go to work with their mom while they go to preschool. She identified the need for more facility dogs and suggested child life as a good fit, as some other pediatric hospitals currently have in place. There is certainly a need for a stronger canine presence in the hospital to help children and their families.

The positive influence of canine companionship is undeniable. I am thankful for all the creatures, who bring us joy, unconditional love, and encourage us through difficult times. Their company is like good medicine.

> "But ask the animals, and they will teach you,
> or the birds in the sky, and they will tell you;
> or speak to the earth, and it will teach you,
> or let the fish in the sea inform you.
> Which of all these does not know that
> the hand of the LORD has done this?
> In his hand is the life of every creature
> and the breath of all mankind.
> *Job 12:7-10*

"I want to have my birthday party here!"

—**A cardiology patient in the playroom**

23.
Matters of the Heart

Sometimes people lose their way but sometimes their journey results in leading them to a greater purpose.

Thomas was a seventeen-year-old boy who overdosed on a combination of illegal drugs and alcohol. As a result, he passed out and fell down a flight of stairs at the drug dealer's house, where he remained lying on his side for two days.

When he didn't return home, his brother, who was also acquainted with drugs and the people who sold them, went looking for him.

I met Thomas after he was admitted to the cardiology unit through the ER. Physically, he appeared very thin and frail and emotionally, he was withdrawn. Medically, he had a range of issues being evaluated and treated, including the loss of mobility in his right arm because he had laid on it for so long. He was weak and confined to a wheelchair.

Socially, he lived in a trailer in a rough part of town with his mom and brothers. He had a probation officer assigned to him due to run-ins with the law. His mom was a single parent with limited cognitive ability, so he was accustomed to taking care of himself.

The hospital was foreign to him and he was newly captive to physical limitations accompanied by pain and weakness. He struggled with hospitalization and initially had difficulty interacting socially with the medical team taking care of him.

The staff was both kind but firm with Thomas who wasn't used to physical limitations or accustomed to respecting authority. Emotionally and developmentally, he was younger than his actual age and staff cared for him with that in mind.

Soon Thomas felt more comfortable with his new surroundings and the structure of a daily schedule that included therapies and meals at consistent times. He was surprised by the compassion and encouragement of the nurses and therapists. They brought him clothes from the hospital clothes closet and some brought him clothes from their homes who had sons the same size.

We began to see more and more of his sweetness and humor but also something else: confidence and hope. We believed in him and he began to believe in himself. When he was seen talking rudely to his mom when she visited, it was made clear to him that he was expected to behave respectfully and politely to her. One day he told me privately, "I'm not used to people being nice to me. I don't know how to handle it."

The matters of life are the matters of the heart. I believe Thomas was better able to follow his heart after it was awakened by the love and care around him, helping him to see possibilities he hadn't realized before.

As Thomas steadily improved, he was transferred from the cardiology unit to the rehab (physical rehabilitation) unit where he had difficulty adjusting to new people and routines. It was requested that I continue providing child life support instead of the rehab child life specialist since it had taken him so long to develop trust with staff.

I was assigned a specific time for intervention each day which we spent in the activity room for teenagers. We listened to music and worked on projects and as we did, Thomas began to open up and talk. He confided that he had never known anyone like the people he had met at the hospital. He began to talk about his hopes and dreams. He said he wanted to graduate from high school, find a good job he liked, get married, and have children.

Thomas told me that a lot of girls liked him but that he didn't have one specific girlfriend. We talked about how easy it is to know a lot of people but it is more important to find one or two that can be trusted. He said that this experience with drugs had taught him, "Don't listen to other people because you want them to like you. Follow your heart."

We live from the inside out. Our internal thought life influences everything else and our beliefs determine the choices we make.

There was a photograph taken of us in the teen room one day before he was discharged. It was one of the last times he needed the assistance of a wheelchair as he gained strength and coordination to walk without assistance. He looked far healthier than the young man I had originally met and much happier and confident, too.

After he was discharged from the hospital, he was required to continue physical and occupational therapy appointments at the hospital's rehab gym. The therapists contacted me as his birthday approached and asked for help celebrating his birthday and decorating the treatment room. We surprised him with a birthday cake and some small birthday presents and he said, "I never thought I'd live to be eighteen." Thomas was released from therapy shortly afterwards.

Tragedy brought him to a place of weakness but love left him with strength and hope.

Spiritual Ink

And now these three remain: faith, hope and love. But the greatest of these is love.
1 Corinthians 13:13

> *"Don't listen to other people because you want them to like you. Follow your heart."*
>
> **—A seventeen-year-old patient**

24.
Mental Jewelry

There is a lot of communication and coordination when patients are moved from one clinical area to another, such as admissions, transfers between medical units, and discharges. People work closely with individuals and teams for a smoother transition and continuity of care.

One day, Heather, a child life specialist who covered the CTICU (Cardiothoracic Intensive Care Unit) updated me on upcoming transfers from the intensive care unit to the cardiology unit I covered. One of the transfers included a baby whose mom was in jail. Heather had worked over the weekend and was able to meet the mom who was allowed to visit before she had to return to jail. It was unknown who the father was.

Heather took the opportunity for memory making activities, taking photos and making scrapbook pages. She took handprints of the baby and as the visit concluded, Heather told the young mom, "This is 'Mental Jewelry.' These memories are yours forever, no one can take these from you."

Plans were made for the baby to be placed in foster care. He was sweet and content during my visits. I was holding him comfortably in my arms when the Resident Physician came to examine the baby prior to discharge. Before the Resident left, he smiled at the baby and said, "Bye buddy, hope you find your dad," which is a line from the movie Elf. There was an unspoken sadness between us about the uncertainty of this child's future.

A short time later, a nurse entered the room, followed by the foster parents. So much communication is nonverbal, but within those initial minutes of interaction, it was clear that the baby boy was going to a good home. She explained the packed bags were hospital gifts of some baby items such as clothes, a baby blanket, and some toys for them to take with them.

When they were finished, I got up from the rocking chair and placed the baby in the arms of his foster mom. They thanked us before they left and as they walked through the door, the nurse and I looked at one another with relief that he was going to a good home.

When someone is sick enough to be hospitalized, they need intervention and the care of others to help them. Hospitals and prisons are very different places but one commonality between them is the need for the involvement of others to help them in the condition they're in. God is a pursuing and redemptive God. I've talked to people involved in prison ministry who have shared stories and accounts of broken lives being turned around.

The mission statement of Jesus can be found in Luke 19:10, "For the Son of Man has come to seek and to save the lost." Seek is an active word which means to look for, search, or pursue. In this passage, Jesus is speaking to a man named Zacchaeus, a Jewish man who was a chief tax collector. Zacchaeus was rich but was despised by the Jews because he collected taxes for Rome. He overcharged the people what was due to pay Rome and collected extra for himself. The Jewish people considered him a traitor. He was not welcome in the Synagogue but he was welcomed by Jesus.

Zacchaeus had heard about Jesus passing through Jericho so he went to see him. Being short in stature, he couldn't see through the crowd so he climbed up a Sycamore tree to get a better view. Zaccheaus went to Jericho to seek Jesus and there he learned that Jesus was also seeking Zaccheaus. As Jesus was passing by, he stopped and called Zaccheaus by name, asking him to come down from the tree so he could stay at his house. That one encounter changed him and Zacchaeus went from being spiritually dead to spiritually alive.

The prophet Ezekiel describes spiritual transformation in Ezekiel 35:26, "I will give you a new heart and put a new spirit in you; I will remove from you your heart of stone and give you a heart of flesh."

God is the Lord Almighty. He can make the impossible possible. God knows where we are today and He sees the future and all that He created us for. Like Zaccheaus, the mom in jail, and the baby in foster care, you and I have a greater destiny to fulfill beyond what we can see or imagine right now. All of our days are before Him.

Jesus came to seek us, to save us, and to heal us in a deep and personal way. "Mental Jewelry" describes our memories with those we love, with both the people we care for and our remembrances of God's intervention and power as He guides us with his love.

Spiritual Ink

Heal me, LORD, and I will be healed; save me and I will be saved, for you are the one I praise.
Jeremiah 17:14

> "I receive more than I give."
>
> —**A hospital volunteer**

25.
A Heart of Compassion

"We're going to enjoy her as long as we have her," said a parent about his baby girl. During the pregnancy, he and his wife learned that their baby would be born with a heart defect. They tried to prepare themselves and their other children for the days ahead as best as they could. Immediately after Lily was born, she was transferred to our children's hospital to be cared for in the CTICU. The first time I met Lily, she was being held by her dad who rocked her in a rocking chair. Her mom was still hospitalized where she had been born. Once she was released from their care, both parents took turns alternating between being at the hospital and at home taking care of their other children.

The parents were both medical professionals on staff at an adult hospital. They were impressed with the care their daughter received in the CTICU and with the hospital as a whole, but they were quite open and articulate about the difficulty of having a sick baby. Neither of them had considered working in pediatrics because it would be too hard, and yet, here they were, struggling as parents of a critically ill child.

Lily's health continued to decline and she became a candidate for a heart transplant. Her parents didn't know what to do. They worried about her quality of life and deliberated about what decisions to make. They weren't always in agreement as either practitioners or parents. They worried about having other children and if the same thing could happen again, even though the condition wasn't genetic. They were hoping for one more child.

They read their Bibles during the long days in the hospital and struggled in prayer. They expressed appreciation for the support they received from their family, friends, and church. The limited time they had together was spent in the CTICU, a room surrounded by glass and in the presence of a large medical staff. They asked lots of questions and researched information. They were tired from stress, lack of sleep, and the demands of caring for their children at home and in the hospital. They spent months waiting for the right "match" while their baby became sicker to the point of finally being vented and sedated. Still, they remained optimistic.

Finally, the long anticipated day arrived when Lily received her new heart. She responded well and began to get stronger and responsive to people, toys, and the world around her. Her older siblings visited the CTICU as she progressed and they looked forward to their baby coming home to live with them.

During a post-transplant cardiac catheterization, I had an opportunity to talk to Lily's dad. He said they were happy to have Lily home, but he knows that new hearts only function for a limited number of years. He knew that other heart transplants would be required in the future and had been talking to some parents whose child had just had his second heart transplant. He also knew that with each surgery came many risks, including the possibility of cognitive skills being compromised. He expressed, as he had in the past, that he wished he could trade places with Lily to spare her from all that she had gone through and all she will go through. He confided that he had found it difficult to return to work in his prior capacity as a nurse with critically-ill patients and was considering other professional opportunities. He told me that while he had always considered himself to have the right priorities, that through this all, he has a deeper understanding of what is really important in this life. He concluded the conversation by saying that Jesus has a heart of compassion for people who are hurting and he, too, feels compassionate in a deeper way than before.

There are lots of answers we won't know on this side of heaven. But when we know our Heavenly Father is with us always and in all circumstances, it is the most important answer of all that we need to know.

> **For he will command his angels concerning you to guard you in all your ways.**
> *Psalm 91:11*

"When we cry, God cries."

—A mom talking to her eight-year-old daughter about her dad's cancer

26.
Betty Crocker

There are a million different ways friendships enrich us. Shared times with others builds connection and brings meaning and appreciation to a time and place, even from days or years past. Moments create memories.

Yesterday thoughts of my friend, Kym, came to mind. We worked together at the hospital at the beginning of our careers before she moved out of state. Kym was a child life specialist on the rehab (rehabilitation) unit. Many of the trauma patients that I worked with in the ER were transferred to the rehab unit where Kym worked with them throughout their often lengthy hospitalization before they were discharged to go home. We worked well together and learned a lot through our clinical experiences.

One of the memories I have of us is when I stopped by the rehab unit one day to see her. As I was approaching the nurse's station where she was charting, a teenaged boy in a wheelchair saw me and called out, "Why are you so ugly?" Everyone at the nurse's station got real quiet, surprised by his question. I smiled in response, restraining my laughter and then he loudly called out, "Psych!!!" and started laughing. The rest of us started laughing, too. He had been flirting with me.

Kym and I decided to become roommates and found an apartment with a good pool. We argued over who would drive the U-Haul on moving day because neither of us were comfortable driving a big truck. I ended up driving and everything was fine. My ER friends helped us move all of our furniture and the day was full of positive energy as new beginnings can bring. It was a good day followed by a good year where Kym and I both met our husbands. I remember the first time she met Ed. She mouthed the words, "He's cute!" to me from across the room.

Yesterday was my husband's birthday which always reminds me of Kym because she witnessed my failed attempts at making Ed an angel food cake, his favorite. After the first cake didn't turn out right, I went back to the grocery store, Big Bear, and bought another boxed mix. That wasn't successful either. I baked it before work and left it to cool. When I got home at midnight, next to the fallen cake I found a note on the kitchen counter from Kym which read, "Yo, Betty, they're $4.99 at Big Bear."

This year I decided to try something new and I made my first lemon meringue pie. It was a win! And I don't know what took me so long to try. I'm still no Betty Crocker but I texted Kym a photo of the pie and she congratulated me and said that angel food cake always reminds her of me. Maybe lemon meringue pie will now do the same.

Many birthdays have been celebrated from that first year until now and lots of other celebrations, too. There are different seasons in life and true living is loving the phase you're in and the people around you, wherever you are on your journey.

Shannon Alford

You make known to me the path of life; you will fill me with joy in your presence, with eternal pleasures at your right hand.
Psalm 16:11

> "He was crying for more chocolate cake. We recently adopted him from Africa and he had never had it before. I only wanted him to have a little bit but he ate it all."
>
> —A dad of a toddler during his first hospitalization

27.
Pray Big

When I worked in the cardiology unit, I came to know some of the patients and families better than others because of long-term or frequent hospitalizations. While I was documenting chart notes at a hallway computer one day, Julia, the mom of a preschooler I knew from previous admissions, saw me and started talking to me. She had a buoyant personality and she and her husband were well-liked by staff.

She asked me how I was doing but my concern was for her. She answered that she was fine and explained they were at the hospital for a heart biopsy. Her son had received a heart transplant as a baby and a few months prior, the doctors were concerned if his body was rejecting the new heart. The issues had resolved and they had been discharged to home, but now they were back for another heart biopsy. Julia said the doctors had a look of concern on their faces when they spoke to her and her husband, which caused her unease. But she had decided that she had two choices: she could either worry about it or pray. She said the worry was negative and made things worse. They had a lot of people praying for them and she could feel it.

Julia and her husband, a pastor, had learned that when they had to come to the hospital or had problems, to communicate to people so they could pray for them because it made a big difference. Julia told me her son's first biopsy was much more difficult emotionally than the heart transplant, even though the heart transplant involves stopping the heart completely for a short period of time. She was surprised how joyful she was on the day of her son's transplant and she credited it to the prayer support. Julia believes in the power of children's prayers and the importance of praying specifically.

According to Julia, it was the hardest thing for her to realize that God loves her children even more than she and her husband do. She sometimes wonders, "Why us?" and I thought she meant she questioned why her son had such complex health issues, but she went on to explain that she wonders why her child got to live when another child did not. When she puts her children to bed every night, she realizes a part of another family is living in their house. She is grateful but feels sorry for that family's loss so that her son's could go on.

Julia stated she realizes this is not the world God intended us to live in. She went on to say that when sin entered the world, Satan was able to bring destruction to this earth and we have also inherited a sinful nature, but it is not what God initially created for us.

When Julia's son was in the CTICU waiting for a heart, she paced the halls and felt she could not continue waiting for months on end. When she returned to her baby's room, she prayed that if it was God's will to take her child, then He would take him, but if he was to get well, then to please answer her prayer quickly. It was only a week and a half later when her son received his new heart.

Julie commented that "out there" it is not popular to talk about faith in God but in the hospital, nobody cares because they think *whatever gets you through.* I think people feel free to share their faith in the hospital because they feel the hope and support of the staff and others around them.

> **Before they call I will answer;**
> **while they are still speaking I will hear.**
> *Isaiah 65:24*

> *"Parents often aren't at their best in the ER."*
>
> —An ER nurse

28.
Flourish

One day as I was walking towards the elevator to go to the cardiology unit, I felt a strong and sudden inclination to take the hallway to my right instead, which led to the cafeteria. I had a lot of patients to see but I decided to trust the leading I was sensing. As soon as I started walking down the hall, I saw a patient and her parents who I had known for a long time. Sarah had undergone extended hospitalizations in her early childhood before she received a kidney transplant. I hadn't seen them in years and Sarah, now a teenager, had come to the hospital for a yearly follow-up. After their morning appointments, they had eaten lunch in the cafeteria and they were hoping to see me. Their next stop was at the child life office to see if I could be paged before they headed back home which was hours away. They had also brought me one of Sarah's school photos. I was so happy to see them, especially with Sarah looking so healthy and full of life.

They were among the many people who had influenced my faith. Sarah had seen angels at her bedside when she was in intensive care and she had parents and grandparents praying for her. I remember her parents spending one of their wedding anniversaries at the hospital and I had been with Sarah during some intense and painful medical interventions. There was a lot of history between us.

When Sarah had to start dialysis three times a week, I tried to stop by once or twice a week to see how she was doing. The dialysis unit at the time was a large room which accommodated five patients and there were curtains that could be drawn for privacy when needed.

The nurses were a small dynamic team of specialized nurses that worked closely together. When they saw how beneficial child life support was for Sarah, they wanted the same for the rest of their patients. They advocated successfully and limited child life coverage was directed to support them, which was more than they had before and it made a big difference in patient care. Resources were made available to them such as coping tools, books, games, and activities. They received resources to celebrate patient birthdays and were included in receiving donations and Christmas gifts for their patients. Sometimes the nurses played bingo with the group of patients during their hours of treatment and they had prizes that patients could choose from a bingo cart.

One of the dialysis nurses and I had a mutual friend who was a child life specialist. The nurse was pregnant and expecting her first child. My child life friend, whose toddler I babysat a few hours a week while she worked, told me that the nurse's babysitter had fallen through at the last minute. She was really worried and didn't know what to do but she still wanted to work two days a week in dialysis. And that's how three beautiful little girls became good friends and their moms did, too. Psalm 32:8 says, "I will instruct you and teach you in the way you should go; I will counsel you with my loving eye on you." That was a wonderful period of time of special friendships. As the girls grew older, my daughter started first grade, my child life friend moved out of town closer to family, my nurse friend had another baby, and I increased my working hours. All along there was flourishing—of health, resources, families, friends, and opportunities, and the journey continued.

> **Surely your goodness and love will follow me all the days of my life, and I will dwell in the house of the LORD forever.**
> *Psalm 23:6*

"They made up their own language. We don't understand what they're saying."

—Parents of three two-year-olds, one they had biologically, one they had planned to adopt, and another upon learning there was another two-year-old in a different part of Africa than the first that also needed a home. The three boys created their own language among them and no one else could understand what they were saying when they talked to one another.

29.
The Journey Onwards

The winds of tomorrow call us forward. I think children tend to be more in tune with God's impartation of knowledge and sense of destiny and I recall moments from my own childhood where I felt an internal stirring of excitement and connection that I didn't understand. I felt that way in kindergarten when I lived next door to my friend, Nan, and she invited me to ride along when her dad drove her mom to work. Her mom was a nurse at a local hospital and I had an understanding that her work was important and a curiosity about what a hospital looked like inside. She had nursing magazines at her house and I remember seeing the cover of one of them with a photograph of a human heart on it. It looked different than I thought it would but I found it interesting. The past influences the future in surprising ways and that introduction to hospital work as a five-year-old was one point of connection among many along the path to working with cardiology patients which I did for most of my career.

When you start aligning with your purpose, the way becomes clearer and opportunities and "coincidences" lead in new directions. Joshua 3:4 says, "Then you will know which way to go, since you have never been this way before." My friend, Janelle, is a child life specialist and we worked together on the cardiology unit. She came over for lunch one day; it had been a long time between visits. One of the things we talked about was how different experiences enlarge your abilities and interests to pursue new projects and passions, yet there's a commonality among them. "It's all connected," said Janelle, and she's right.

Our journey of life is also connected to other people. There have been those who have come before us and accomplished great things and there are others who come after us to do the same. The patient rooms where Janelle and I once spent so much time taking care of patients are now the same rooms that my niece, a nursing student, cares for patients. After she graduates from nursing school in the spring, she will work there full- time. It's all connected. Life is a moving forward adventure and there's still more yet to come!

**Your eyes saw my unformed body;
all the days ordained for me were written in your
book before one of them came to be.**
Psalm 139:16

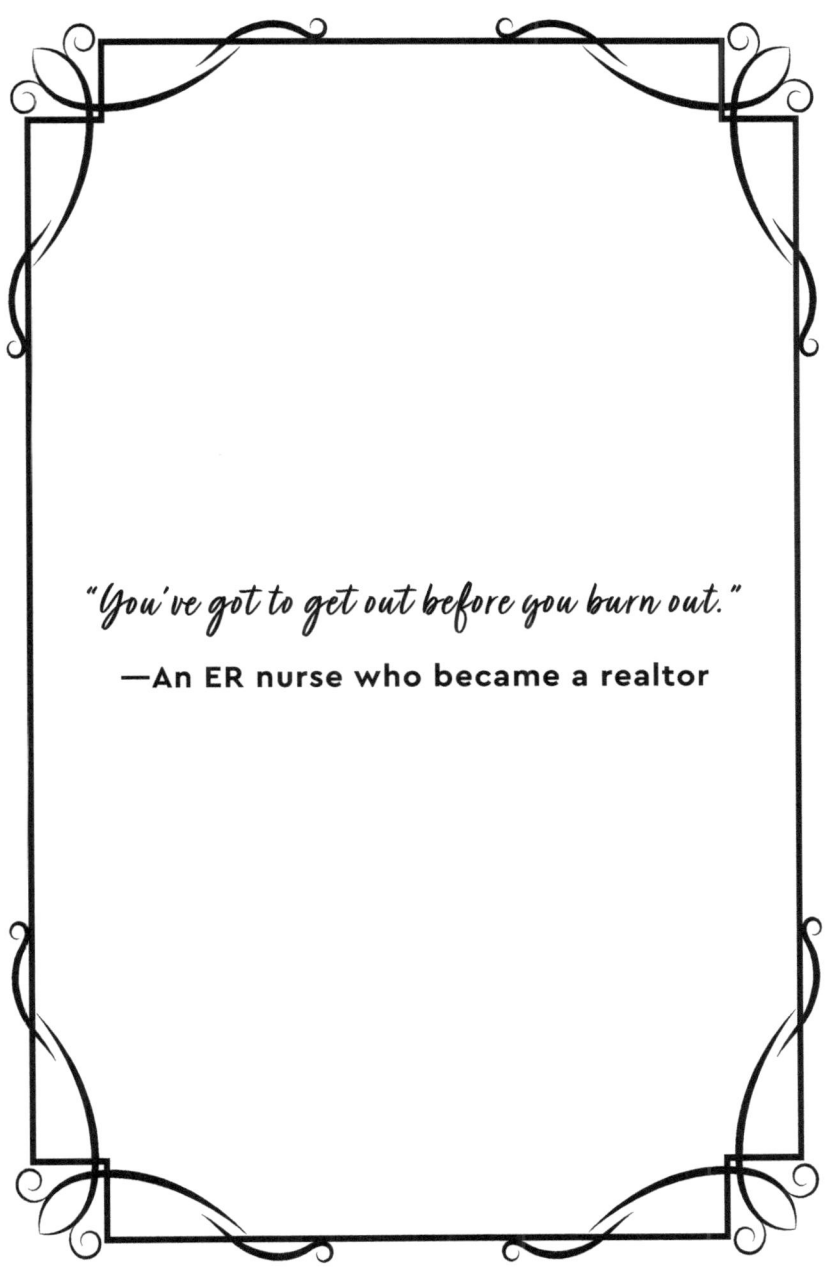

"You've got to get out before you burn out."

—An ER nurse who became a realtor

30.
Child Life Bro

The son of a child life specialist asked her why the title was called that name and she answered, "I don't know, what do you think it should be called, child life bro?" That makes me laugh but as teachers, healers, and encouragers, we, like other healthcare workers, "help a brother in need." 1 Peter 4:10 says, "As each has received a gift, use it to serve one another, as good stewards of God's varied grace."

In a scheduled playgroup for young children held by child life and early intervention staff, only one child and parent attended one day. The early intervention teacher interacted with the three-year-old patient while his mom and I sat across the room quietly talking at one of the children's activity tables. She explained that she and her husband had grown children and were grandparents. They had lived in a house in the country and had a nice life but they were bored. They decided to start a non-profit organization helping those in need, which ultimately prompted them to move to the city and adopt four siblings. The three-year-old was the youngest and he had heart issues that went untreated before his adoption. They moved to a house that had drug dealers and prostitutes at nearby street corners and opened their home every Saturday to welcome children and neighbors, providing activities for kids and feeding both the young and old. They were known to the neighborhood as Grandma and Grandpa. They grew to partner with organizations to provide food and Christmas presents to families and they started a home for pregnant teenagers who had nowhere to go. I was amazed at her passion and drive. As playgroup ended, we walked toward the elevator to return to the cardiology unit. She turned to me and said, "I always think about Matthew 5:16 in the Bible which says to let your light shine before men because it brings glory to God." Matthew 25:40 also says, "Truly I tell you, whatever you did for one of the least of these brothers and sisters of mine, you did for me." Children are vulnerable and are among the "least of these."

It's a dark world out there, but light shines in the darkness. Light shines; it illuminates and creates change. Jesus is the light of the world and we are the way He has chosen to reveal Himself to a hurting world around us.

When my daughter was six, she broke her arm while she was at a soccer game with my husband, who was a coach. I was scheduled to work in the ER that day so I stayed home to get ready. Instead of working as staff, I was a parent of a hurt child in the ER that day. Audrey needed surgery and was admitted overnight. She missed the last days of of the school year and we had to reschedule her birthday party which was a pool party, until her cast came off. She saw and felt the concern of her caregivers. She said to me, "Your friends in the hospital are really nice to kids. I'm glad you work there." I'm glad I did, too. We are made to live in a community. As I once heard someone say, "When your hands are open to give, they're open to receive." A hospital volunteer told me, "I receive more than I give." That is the blessing of love. It opens spiritual eyes and softens hearts to accomplish great things that nothing else could. May you enjoy your life as we're meant to do. Take good care of the people and pets around you, and let your light shine brightly!

> **Surely your goodness and love will follow me all the days of my life, and I will dwell in the house of the LORD forever.**
> *Psalm 23:6*

"Hospital work is hard work and not only is it hard work, but it's also heart work."

—A child life specialist

About the Author

Shannon Alford writes to encourage others through her humor, inspiration, and faith. She is a Child Life Specialist with over twenty years of experience working at a pediatric hospital helping children and families struggling with trauma, illness, and loss. She loves writing, encouraging others in their creative pursuits, and spending time with her family and two rescue dogs.

Suggested companion guide from the author

Available worldwide wherever you buy your books!

www.ingramcontent.com/pod-product-compliance
Lightning Source LLC
Chambersburg PA
CBHW061808070526
44586CB00024B/2766